MISSIONAL
ECCLESIOLOGY

A. Blake White

Other Books by A. Blake White

The Newness of the New Covenant
The Law of Christ: A Theological Proposal
Galatians: A Theological Interpretation
Abide in Him: A Theological Interpretation of John's First Letter
Union with Christ: Last Adam & Seed of Abraham
What is New Covenant Theology? An Introduction
Theological Foundations for New Covenant Ethics
The Abrahamic Promises in the Book of Galatians

MISSIONAL ECCLESIOLOGY

A. Blake White

5317 Wye Creek Drive, Frederick, MD 21703-6938
301-473-8781 | info@newcovenantmedia.com
www.NewCovenantMedia.com

Missional Ecclesiology

Printed in the United States of America

ISBN 13: 978-1-928965-56-5

To Jason Arnold:

I am looking forward to seeing how God uses you to embody this kind of ecclesiology.
May He be pleased to use you to draw many sheep into His fold.

Table of Contents

INTRODUCTION

Before making a case for a missional ecclesiology, I need to say that mission is not the *only* thing that needs to be emphasized today. It is *vital*, but there are plenty of other ecclesiological areas we could spend our time thinking about. There are other vital elements as well that would be worth reflecting upon, such as worship, doctrine, preaching, nurture, and love. Some circles may overemphasize mission and neglect other areas, but there are also many congregations that neglect mission. So although there are many aspects to talk about, I think this is a neglected one, and I want to issue a call to reshape our ecclesiology to be more mission-driven. Evangelicals can tend to become inward-focused. As Stott says, there is always a strong tendency to "withdraw into a kind of closed, evangelical, monastic community."[1] We must fight against this tendency with a robust understanding of the nature of the new covenant community.

What is Missional?

What, then, does the term "missional" mean anyway? It can seem that there are as many definitions as there are definers.[2] To complicate matters, there have been a dozen

---

[1] John Stott, *Motives and Methods in Evangelism* (Leicester, UK: Inter-Varsity, 1962), 14.

[2] See Timothy Keller, *Center Church* (Grand Rapids: Zondervan, 2012), 256-58 for four streams of the missional movement. Though diverse, Keller points out the four points common to each stream: all agree we now live in a post-Christendom age; all recognize that all too often the church has been culturally captive; all believe that mission is

books a year published in the last fifteen years with the word "missional" in the title.[3] The term has been a buzzword for many within the "emerging church."[4] Now, many will be tempted to automatically dismiss any merit in the term. "Guilt by association with the guilty," but genetic fallacies aside, surely the charitable and wise thing to do is to ask and examine whether or not these emerging leaders can teach us anything.[5] Among other things, the emerging movement is protesting the church's blind captivity to Enlightenment rationalism, its typically narrow view of salvation, requiring belief before belonging, un-contextualized worship, ineffective preaching, weak ecclesiology, and tribalism.[6] Mark Driscoll, controversial-yet-never-boring pastor of Mars Hill Church in Seattle, defines the emerging church as "a growing, loosely connected movement of primarily young pastors who are glad to see the end of modernity and

more than merely a department of the church and that we are all sent out to be a blessing; all call the church to be a contrast community.

[3] Keller, _Center Church,_ 251.

[4] Many use the term to speak of cultural transformation, usually tied to Kuyperian philosophy. To use Richard Niebuhr's well-known typology, most missional thinkers would probably hold to the "Christ the transformer of culture" model. I will not be using the term in this way.

[5] For a critique of the emerging church movement, see Kevin DeYoung and Ted Kluck, _Why We're Not Emergent_ (Chicago: Moody, 2008) and although dated, see D.A. Carson, _Becoming Conversant with the Emerging Church_ (Grand Rapids: Zondervan, 2005).

[6] Jim Belcher, _Deep Church: A Third Way Beyond Emerging and Traditional_ (Downers Grove, IL: IVP Books, 2009), 40-43.

are seeking to function as missionaries who bring the gospel of Jesus Christ to emerging and postmodern cultures."[7]

It is this notion of "seeking to function as missionaries" that I want to focus on in this book. I will use the term "missional" simply as "an adjective denoting something that is related to or characterized by mission."[8] Missiologist Eddie Gibbs is helpful for clarifying what the term means:

> The term missional, which we are using in relation to churches in North America and other parts of the Western world, draws attention to the essential nature and vocation of the church as God's called and sent people. It sees the church primarily as the instrument of God's mission. Following Lesslie Newbigin and others, a church that is missional understands that God's mission calls and sends the church of Jesus Christ to be a missionary church in its own society and in the cultures in which it finds itself.9

The point is not to describe an activity of the church, but its essence and identity.[10] We must have a biblically-informed self-understanding before we get busy with all sorts of potentially wrongheaded activity.[11] In short, theo-

---

[7] Mark Driscoll, *Confessions of a Reformission Rev* (Grand Rapids: Zondervan, 2006), 22.

[8] Christopher J.H. Wright, *The Mission of God: Unlocking the Bible's Grand Narrative* (Downers Grove, IL: IVP Academic, 2006), 24.

[9] Eddie Gibbs, *ChurchNext* (Downers Grove, IL: IVP Books, 2000), 51.

[10] Michael W. Goheen, *A Light to the Nations: The Missional Church and the Biblical Story* (Grand Rapids: Baker Academic, 2011), 4; Gregg R. Allison, *Sojourners and Strangers: The Doctrine of the Church* (Wheaton, IL: Crossway, 2012), 147.

[11] Craig Van Gelder, *The Essence of the Church: A Community Created by the Spirit* (Grand Rapids: Baker, 2000), 38.

logical identity must precede ecclesial activity.[12] George Hunsberger correctly suggests there is "a lack of theological depth regarding how churches think about their identity and how they relate to the cultural context."[13] I, for one, think some of these emerging prophets are on to something here. I agree with many who think that the current church in North America needs a fresh dose of ecclesiology. Mission - local and beyond - should be seen as vitally important to any biblically-driven ecclesiology. As Swiss Theologian Emil Brunner famously put it, "The Church exists by mission, just as a fire exists by burning. Where there is no mission, there is no Church."[14] So, a missional church sees the entire congregation as a body *sent to the world* and existing not for itself but to bring the gospel of Jesus to the lost world.[15] I do think that "missional" as distinct but related to "missionary" is proving its worth today as churches better understand their place and role in redemptive history,[16] but if you get hung up on terms, disregard it and come up with another.[17]

---

[12] Ross Hastings, *Missional God, Missional Church* (Downers Grove: IVP Academic, 2012), 259.

[13] George R. Hunsberger and Craig Van Gelder, eds., *The Church Between Gospel and Culture* (Grand Rapids: Eerdmans, 1996), 1.

[14] Emil Brunner, *The Word and the World* (London: Student Christian Movement Press, 1931), 108.

[15] Goheen, *A Light to the Nations,* 4.

[16] Alan Kreider and Eleanor Kreider, *Worship & Mission After Christendom* (Scottdale, PA: Herald Press, 2011), 45.

[17] See the concerned Kevin DeYoung and Greg Gilbert in *What is the Mission of the Church?* (Wheaton, IL: Crossway, 2011), 20-27. One could opt for "missiological ecclesiology," but this is a tad more cumbersome than "missional ecclesiology" in my opinion.

It will be helpful to understand a little history before we look at the church's call to a missional vocation.

PART I –
SECULAR HISTORY

The Fall of the Church[18]

As the New Testament makes clear, Christianity started small. Many in the Roman Empire thought it was merely a sect within Judaism. The church remained relatively obscure and certainly marginalized for the first 300 years of her existence, but experienced a dramatic shift in the 4th Century. She went from being a sporadically persecuted fringe movement to the dominant religion of the Roman Empire. The persecuted became the persecutors. How did such a dramatic shift occur? The story goes that one Gaius Flavius Valerius Aurelius Constantinus (aka Constantine) saw a vision of a *chi rho* (or a cross depending on which version of the story you read) in the sky circled by a rainbow forming the message "With This Conquer" (*entoutōnika*).[19] Later that night the risen Christ made a personal visit to Constantine

---

[18] See Franklin H. Littell, *The Anabaptist View of the Church* (Paris, AK: The Baptist Standard Bearer, 1958), 46-78.

[19] Bryan M. Litfin, "Eusebius on Constantine: Truth and Hagiography at the Milvian Bridge," *JETS* 55, no. 4 (December 2012), 775. It is strange indeed that the Christ who called his followers to turn the other cheek and to love their enemies would tell an emperor to conquer by the cross. As Shane Claiborne and Chris Haw write, "Hmm … ironic, considering that for Jesus the cross meant refusal of worldly ways of conquering." Shane Claiborne and Chris Haw, *Jesus For President* (Grand Rapids: Zondervan, 2008), 162.

and told him to make a battle standard (a labarum). It is worth noting that earlier in his life, Constantine had also received a visit from Apollo (son of Zeus) that helped him overcome Maximian and other victories as well.[20] On October 28, 312 AD, Constantine defeated Maxentius to win the West at the Battle of the Milvian Bridge. Constantine's admirer and hagiographer Eusebius, who wrote *The Life of Constantine* in 339, two years after his death, would see this battle as the decisive victory for the Christian faith. In the author's opinion, it is highly unlikely that Constantine was genuinely converted. Rather, he was probably an extremely shrewd politician who knew how to unite the Empire in the name of religion. Three years after the vision of Christ the Arch of Constantine was erected in 315, and was full of pagan imagery. *Sol Invictus* (a reference to the unconquered sun god) continued to appear on Roman coins until 325.[21] Historian Justo Gonzàles surmises that

> Constantine seems to have thought that the Unconquered Sun and the Christian God were compatible – perhaps two views of the same Supreme Deity – and that other gods, although subordinate, were nevertheless real and relatively powerful. Thus, on occasion, he would consult the oracle of Apollo, accept the title of High Priest that had traditionally been the prerogative of emperors, and partake of all sorts of pagan ceremonies without thinking that he was thus betraying or abandoning the God who had given him victory and power.[22]

---

[20] Litfin, "Eusebius on Constantine," 781.

[21] Litfin, "Eusebius on Constantine," 779 n. 28.

[22] Justo L. Gonzàles, *The Story of Christianity,* Vol. 1 (Peabody, MA: Prince, 2005), 122.

He never placed himself under the direction of Christian leaders; he determined his own religious practices; he repeatedly participated in pagan rites long after his "conversion;" he continued to serve other gods and functioned as the high priest of paganism his whole life, and he wasn't baptized until on his deathbed[23] – seemingly merely in order to ensure all his bases were covered.

Michael Frost and Alan Hirsch, co-authors of *The Shaping of Things to Come* note, "Constantine came to the throne of the Roman Empire and granted Christians complete freedom of worship and even favored Christianity, thereby undermining all other religions in the empire. In virtually an instant, Christianity moved from being a marginalized, subversive, and persecuted movement secretly gathering in houses and catacombs to being the favored religion in the empire. Everything changed!"[24] In AD 380, Theodosius made it the official religion of the Roman Empire;[25] in the sixth century, Emperor Justinian the First made baptism into the Triune name compulsory![26] Talk about a church growth strategy! Just imagine how drastically things changed. Now,

---

[23] Ibid., 121-23.

[24] Michael Frost and Alan Hirsch, *The Shaping of Things to Come: Innovation and Mission for the 21st-Century Church* (Peabody, MA: Hendrickson, 2003), 8. Alister E. McGrath notes that the edict issued by Galerius in 311 to stop the persecution of Christians "explicitly identified Christianity as a religion, and offered it the full protection of the law. The legal status of Christianity, which had been ambiguous up to this point, was now resolved. The church no longer existed under a siege mentality," *Historical Theology* (Malden, MA: Blackwell, 1998), 19-20.

[25] Goheen, *A Light to the Nations*, 9.

[26] Kreider and Kreider, *Worship & Mission*, 38.

to be a member of society was to be a member of the church. To say that ecclesiological identity was negatively impacted would be a major understatement. The salt became tasteless and the light was dimmed.

Many consider this period to be the "fall of the church." This new favored civil status[27] of Christianity led to what has been known as Christendom (Christ's kingdom): the idea of a state church that would eventually lead to the Holy Roman Empire in AD 800.[28] Christendom is that period in history when the church assumed influence by its connection to secular power.[29] Stuart Murray describes it as follows:

> Christendom was a geographical region in which almost everyone was at least nominally Christian.
>
> Christendom was a historical era resulting from the fourth-century conversion of Constantine and lasting into the late twentieth century.
>
> Christendom was a civilization decisively shaped by the story, language, symbols, and rhythms of Christianity.
>
> Christendom was a political arrangement in which church and state provided mutual, if often uneasy, support and legitimation.
>
> Christendom was an ideology, a mindset, a way of thinking about God's activity in the world.[30]

---

[27] D.A. Carson, *The Gagging of God* (Grand Rapids: Zondervan, 1996), 343.

[28] Douglas A. Sweeney, *The American Evangelical Story* (Grand Rapids: Baker, 2005), 188-89.

[29] Frost and Hirsch, *The Shaping of Things to Come*, 15.

[30] Stuart Murray, *The Naked Anabaptist: The Bare Essentials of a Radical Faith* (Scottdale, PA: Herald Press, 2010), 73.

In many ways, the church in the West has been functioning under the Christendom model from the fourth century to the twentieth century. Whatever its undoubted benefits, it seems to me and many others that when the church came from the margins to the center of the Roman Empire, mission was left at the margins.

Reformation

God used the Reformation in major ways to bring the gospel to light after years of darkness. There was a recovery of the authority of Scripture, justification by faith, the priesthood of all believers (in theory, anyway), and many other glorious doctrines that Protestants largely take for granted now. But not all Reformation theology is gospel. Lesslie Newbigin writes:

> That conception [corpus Christianum, i.e., Christendom] is the background of all the Reformation theologies. They take it for granted. They are set not in a missionary situation but in this situation in which Christendom is taken for granted. This means that in their doctrines of the church they are defining their position over against one another within the context of the corpus Christianum. They are not defining the Church as over against a pagan world. It is not necessary to point out how profoundly this affects the structure of their thinking.[31]

One of the ecclesiological teachings that emerged from the Reformation was the identification of the "marks" of the church. These marks were to distinguish the true churches

---

[31] Lesslie Newbigin, *Household of God* (New York: Friendship Press, 1954), 1-2; Littell, *The Anabaptist View of the Church*, 109-37.

from false churches.[32] There were primarily three ecclesiological marks stemming from the reformation: true preaching of the Word (i.e., pure doctrine), biblical administration of the sacraments, and the exercise of church discipline.[33] These marks *are* rooted in Scripture and *need* to be present for a true church. The problem arose from the way people began to view the church because of these marks. The emphasis on the marks of the church shifted the focus from the identity of the church to the function of the church.[34] We have inherited a view of the church as a *place* where certain things take place and where certain marks are present.[35] The idea that the church is a place or building was foreign to the writers of the New Testament. Today, it is common to talk as if the church were a building. The pastor welcomes the congregation with: "Isn't it good to be in the house of God this morning?" We ask, "Where do you *go to* church?" Most people assume the church is a place where things happen. In the minds of too many, the church has become a vendor of religious goods rather than the blood-bought, Spirit-filled community of King Jesus.[36]

Post-Christendom

---

[32] John M. Frame, *Salvation Belongs to the Lord: An Introduction to Systematic Theology* (Phillipsburg, NJ: P & R Publishing, 2006), 241.

[33] Van Engen, *God's Missionary People*, 36.

[34] Van Gelder, *The Essence of the Church*, 57.

[35] George R. Hunsberger, "Sizing Up the Shape of the Church," in *The Church Between Gospel & Culture: The Emerging Mission in North America*, eds. George R. Hunsberger and Craig Van Gelder (Grand Rapids: Eerdmans, 1996), 337.

[36] Hunsberger, "Missional Vocation," 83-84.

Christendom is over, or is at least shattering to pieces all around us. The day of a "churched culture" is over.[37] Darrell Guder, Professor of Missional and Ecumenical Theology at Princeton Theological Seminary, notes that "while modern missions have led to an expansion of world Christianity, Christianity in North America has moved (or been moved) away from its position of dominance as it has experienced the loss not only of numbers but of power and influence within society."[38] America is no longer a Christian nation, if it ever was one.[39] D.A. Carson writes,

> A mere quarter of a century ago, if we were dealing with an atheist, he or she was not a generic atheist but a Christian atheist — that is, the God he or she did not believe in was more or

---

[37] Hunsberger, "The Newbigin Gauntlet: Developing a Domestic Missiology for North America," 17. Stetzer writes, "Christendom has come to an end. No longer is Christianity the 'chaplain' to the broader culture. Christianity was universally assumed as the American religion even though it was not widely embraced. It was once perceived as part of our national ethos. No longer can that claim be made. This 'humiliation' of Christendom has been underway for two centuries. It is no longer appropriate, if it ever was, to speak of 'Christian America'." *Planting New Churches in a Postmodern Age* (Nashville: Broadman & Holman, 2003), 14.

[38] Darrell L. Guder, "Missional Church: From Sending to Being Sent," in *Missional Church: A Vision for the Sending of the church in North America*, ed. Darrell L. Guder (Grand Rapids: Eerdmans, 1998), 1.

[39] On this debated question, see the recent volume *Christian America: Perspectives on Our Religious Heritage,* ed. Daryl C. Cornett (Nashville: B&H Academic, 2011); Cf. also Richard T. Hughes, *Christian America and the Kingdom of God* (Chicago: University of Illinois Press, 2009); Gregory A. Boyd, *The Myth of a Christian Nation* (Grand Rapids: Zondervan, 2005).

less a god of discernibly Judeo-Christian provenance. The athe-
ist was not particularly denying the existence of Hindu gods—
Krishna, perhaps—but the God of the Bible. But that meant
that the categories were still ours. The domain of discourse was
ours.[40]

Carson writes elsewhere that "Oprah shapes more of the nation's grasp of right and wrong than most of the pulpits in
the land."[41]

Some have speculated that America is "the most diverse
nation in the world."[42] David Wells writes that "America has
become a truly multiethnic society and perhaps the most re-
ligiously diverse one in the world. The exotic religions from
faraway places that once only filled pages of _National Geo-
graphic_ may now be found next door. Mosques, landmarks
that once seemed confined to the Middle East, can now be
seen side by side with churches in America, though much of
the practice of Islam is also invisible to most people."[43] Wells
continues:

> Today's immigration is creating a multiethnic society, and
> this, in turn, has contributed to the extraordinary religious plu-
> ralism which has emerged, because many of the new immi-
> grants are at least formally religious and some of their religions

---

[40] D. A. Carson, ed., _Telling the Truth_ (Grand Rapids: Zondervan, 2000),
384.

[41] D. A. Carson, _The Gagging of God_, 24.

[42] Ed Stetzer and David Putman, _Breaking the Missional Code: Your Church
Can Become a Missionary in Your Community_ (Nashville: Broadman &
Holman, 2006), 14.

[43] David Wells, _Above All Earthly Pow'rs: Christ in a Postmodern World_
(Grand Rapids: Eerdmans, 2005), 5.

are relatively new to America ... Indeed, it would probably be true to say that the context in which Christian faith now finds itself is, from an ethnic and religious angle, more like the century in which the New Testament was written than, say, the nineteenth century in America or, for that matter, Europe. Missionaries once went overseas to work among peoples from other cultures and religions. Now, some of those people are making their way into Western cities and universities and some are from places to which missionaries can gain little or no access... European and American missionaries went out into the world; part of the world is now coming to the missionaries.[44]

I have already mentioned the name Lesslie Newbigin a couple of times. He was the first major "prophet" to start sounding the alarm. He is hugely influential in the missional church movement. George Hunsberger can even speak of the "Newbigin Gauntlet," referring to his calling for a missiology for the West. He writes, "In effect, he has thrown down the gauntlet, challenging the churches of the West to look to our own contexts as missionary settings and to be as rigorous about what that must mean for our own missionary life as we have been about mission done elsewhere."[45] You know he has something to say when he is quoted by the likes of Tim Keller, Michael Horton,[46] Mark Driscoll,[47] Brian

---

[44] Ibid., 95. D.A. Carson similarly notes that, "as much of Western culture increasingly distances itself from its Judeo-Christian roots, the task of evangelism takes on the overtones of a missionary enterprise to an alien culture." *The Gagging of God*, 491.

[45] George R. Hunsberger, "The Newbigin Gauntlet: Developing a Domestic Missiology for North America," in Hunsberger and Van Gelder, eds., *The Church Between Gospel and Culture*, 6.

[46] Michael Horton, *The Gospel Commission* (Grand Rapids: Baker Books, 2011), 6.

McLaren,[48] and John Armstrong.[49] Newbigin was born in England, trained at Cambridge, and then appointed to be a missionary by the Church of Scotland in South India in 1936. He returned to England in 1959 where he led the ecumenical movement in various capacities. He was a key person in the founding of the World Council of Churches. Like Karl Barth, he is not an evangelical but is quite critical of liberalism and has much to teach us. When he returned to England from the mission field, it had become a different place, but the churches were "doing business as usual" and he began to call for a missionary church in the West. His last twenty years proved to be of most lasting influence through his writings.[50] He argued that the West was not a secular society

---

[47] Mark Driscoll, _The Radical Reformission: Reaching Out Without Selling Out_ (Grand Rapids: Zondervan, 2004), 19.

[48] E.g., Brian D. McLaren, _A Generous Orthodoxy_ (Grand Rapids: Zondervan, 2004), 115-25.

[49] John H. Armstrong, _Your Church is Too Small_ (Grand Rapids: Zondervan, 2010), 158-60, where he says he has been most influenced by Newbigin. I am dependent on Armstrong for the biographical information.

[50] See _The Other Side of 1984_ (Grand Rapids: Eerdmans, 1983); _Foolishness to the Greeks_ (Grand Rapids: Eerdmans, 1986); _The Gospel in a Pluralist Society_ (Grand Rapids: Eerdmans, 1989); _Truth to Tell_ (Grand Rapids: Eerdmans, 1991). David Bosch builds off of Newbigin, and Darrell Guder builds off of both Bosch and Newbigin. Two foundational academic books building off of Newbigin are _The Church Between Gospel and Culture,_ eds. George R. Hunsberger and Craig Van Gelder (Grand Rapids: Eerdmans, 1996) and _Missional Church: A Vision for the Sending of the Church in North America_, ed. Darrell Guder (Grand Rapids: Eerdmans, 1998).

without God but a pagan society full of idols.[51] The West is now a mission field.

---

[51] See *Open Secret*, 8; Keller, *Center Church*, 253. The autonomy of human reason was seen as one of the biggest idols in post-Enlightenment North America.

PART II – REDEMPTIVE HISTORY

We now turn from secular history to redemptive history. To speak of redemptive history is to speak of God's redemptive actions throughout history, which is another way of speaking of the *Missio Dei* (Latin for the mission of God). The term *"Missio Dei"* was first used in 1952 at a missionary conference in Willingen, Germany by Karl Hartenstein. He was building off of the theology of Karl Barth and his view of God's actions in the world.[52]

The Bible records for us the mission of God. Mission is first and foremost not the church's; it is God's. This is why Luke is careful to say that *the Lord added* to the church in the book of Acts (Acts 2:47, 5:14, 11:24). In this sense, the whole Bible is a missional document. As Ralph Winter puts it, "The Bible is not the basis of missions; missions is the basis of the Bible."

In their book on a biblical theology of mission, Andreas Köstenberger and Peter T. O'Brien write, "God's saving plan for the whole world forms a grand frame around the entire story of Scripture. His mission is bound up with his salvation which moves from creation to new creation."[53] A fun-

---

[52] Kreider and Kreider, *Worship & Mission*, 44; Van Gelder, *The Essence of the Church*, 33; Keller, *Center Church*, 251; Wright, *The Mission of God*, 62.

[53] Andreas J. Köstenberger and Peter T. O'Brien, *Salvation to the Ends of the Earth: A Biblical Theology of Mission* (Downers Grove, IL: InterVar-

damental reason the church should be missional is because her God is missional. He is a missionary God.[54]

The Father chooses and gives to the Son (John 10:29) who redeems, and the Father through the Son sends the Spirit to apply the blessings of the age to come, won by the Son for his sheep. Then the Son commissions those sheep to gather in the scattered exiles, all in anticipation of the renewal of the cosmos (Rom 8). God is a missionary God. It is not so much that God's church has a mission but that God's mission has a church. Mission was not made for the church but the church was made for God's mission.[55] God sends the church because he is already on a mission. "The church does not simply have a missions department; it should wholly exist *to be* a mission."[56] The covenant community is the instrument of the mission of God.

---

sity Press, 2001), 263; see also Gregg R. Allison, *Sojourners and Strangers* (Wheaton, IL: Crossway, 2012), 141.

[54] Tim Chester and Steve Timmis, *Total Church* (Wheaton, IL: Crossway, 2008), 105; Kreider and Kreider, *Worship & Mission*, 44-45; Van Gelder, *The Essence of the Church*, 30, 96-97; Köstenberger and O'Brien, *Salvation to the Ends of the Earth,* 52, 269; John R. Franke, *The Character of Theology* (Grand Rapids: Baker Academic, 2005), 68, 184.

[55] http://www.missionalmanifesto.net/. Accessed 12/17/12; Jurgen Moltmann, "The Church in the Power of the Spirit," trans. Margaret Kohl (New York: Harper & Row, 1977), 10. Wright, *The Mission of God*, 62.

[56] Keller, *Center Church*, 251.

Creation

When God created, he had the new creation in mind. His mission starts here. He creates man and commissions him to rule. Adam is kingly. This royal figure is commissioned to "work" and "keep" the garden (Gen 2:15), verbs that when used together later in the Hebrew Bible refer to the work of priests (Num 3:7-8, 8:25-26, 18:5-6).[57] Therefore, he is a king with priestly duties. He is the prototypical king-priest called to serve God in the garden-temple.[58] G.K. Beale writes, "The intention seems to be that Adam was to widen the boundaries of the Garden in ever increasing circles by extending the border of the Garden sanctuary into the inhospitable outer spaces. The outward expansion would include the goal of spreading the glorious presence of God."[59] Therefore, Genesis 1:28 with the command to 'Be fruitful and multiply and fill the earth and subdue it and have dominion' can be seen as "the first 'Great Commission' that was repeatedly applied to humanity as history progressed."[60] Of course we know that another Adam is needed to fulfill God's mission since the first one failed miserably by attempting to live autono-

[57] T. Desmond Alexander, *From Eden to the New Jerusalem* (Downers Grove, IL: InterVarsity Press, 2008), 22-23.

[58] G.K. Beale, *The Temple and the Church's Mission: A biblical theology of the dwelling place of God* (Downers Grove, IL: InterVarsity Press, 2004), 66-80. Also cf. idem, "Eden, the Temple, and the Church's Mission in the New Creation," JETS 48.1 (March 2005): 5-31; Peter J. Gentry, "Kingdom Through Covenant: Humanity as the Divine Image," The Southern Baptist Journal of Theology 12.1 (Spring 2008): 37-39.

[59] Beale, *The Temple and the Church's Mission*, 85.

[60] Ibid., 117.

mously.[61] The garden-temple they were called to protect now has to be protected from them![62] Although not outside of God's plan, this "cosmic tragedy"[63] changed the way God would fulfill his mission on earth. Rather than honoring and giving thanks to the Creator, now all of humanity outside of Christ exchanges the glory of God for created things (Rom 1:21-23). Now a missional ecclesiology "exists because worship doesn't."[64]

Abraham[65]

Genesis 3-11 are dark chapters. God floods the earth and starts afresh with Noah, but Noah is "in Adam" and follows in his footsteps by overindulging in the fruit (of the vine). Then we have the tower builders and the beginning of the Age of Enlightenment. What will God do now? Christopher Wright, in his superb book *The Mission of God*, writes,

> What can God do next? Something that only God could have thought of. He sees an elderly, childless couple in the land of Babel and decides to make them the fountain head, the launch pad of his whole mission of cosmic redemption. We can

---

[61] Craig G. Bartholomew and Michael W. Goheen, *The Drama of Scripture* (Grand Rapids: Baker Academic, 2004), 43.

[62] Sandra L. Richter, *The Epic of Eden* (Downers Grove, IL: IVP Academic, 2008), 112.

[63] Stephen G. Dempster, *Dominion and Dynasty: A Theology of the Hebrew Bible* (Downers Grove, IL: InterVarsity Press, 2003), 66.

[64] John Piper, *Let the Nations Be Glad: The Supremacy of God in Missions* (Grand Rapids: Baker Books, 1993), 11; Goheen, *A Light to the Nations*, 46.

[65] This section is taken from my book *The Abrahamic Promises in the Book of Galatians* (Frederick, MD: New Covenant Media, forthcoming).

almost hear the sharp intake of breath among the heavenly
hosts when the astonishing plan was revealed. They knew, as
the reader of Genesis 1-11 now knows, the sheer scale of devas-
tation that serpentine evil and human recalcitrance have
wrought in God's creation. What sort of an answer can be pro-
vided through Abram and Sarai? Yet that is precisely the scale
of what now follows. The call of Abram is the beginning of
God's answer to the evil of human hearts, the strife of nations
and the groaning brokenness of his whole creation. A new
world, ultimately a new creation, begins in this text. But it is a
new world that bursts out of the womb of the old – the old
world portrayed in Genesis 1-11.[66]

According to a rabbinic midrash on Genesis, God says, "I
will make Adam first and if he goes astray I will send Abraham to sort it out."[67] Darrell Bock and Craig Blaising write,
"The Abrahamic covenant consequently sets forth the foundational relationship between God and all humankind from
Abraham onward. This means that to understand the Bible,
one must read it in view of the Abrahamic covenant, for that
covenant with Abraham is the foundational framework for
interpreting the Scripture and the history of redemption
which it reveals."[68]

---

[66] Wright, *The Mission of God*, 199-200.

[67] *Gen. Rab.* 14:6 quoted in Goheen, *A Light to the Nations*, 27.

[68] Craig A. Blaising and Darrell L. Bock, *Progressive Dispensationalism*
(Grand Rapids: Baker Books, 2000), 135. Stephen J. Wellum agrees,
writing, "Scripture presents the Abrahamic covenant as the basis for
all God's dealings with the human race and the backbone for understanding the biblical covenants. Truly, it is through Abraham and his
seed—ultimately viewed in terms of our Lord Jesus Christ (Gal
3:16)—that our triune God fulfills his eternal purpose and promise to
save a people for himself and to usher in a new creation. This is borne

Take note of the structure of these important verses:

   I. Go to the land I will show you

      A. I will make you into a great nation[69]

      B. I will bless you

      C. I will make your name great

   II. Be a blessing[70]

      A. I will bless those who bless you

      B. I will curse whoever curses you

---

out, not only in terms of OT theology, but also in how the NT authors interpret the fulfillment of the Abrahamic promise in light of the person and work of Christ (e.g., Romans 4 and Galatians 3)," in his programmatic essay "Baptism and the Relationship Between the Covenants," 128-29, 132 in *Believer's Baptism,* eds. Thomas R. Schreiner and Shawn D. Wright (Nashville, B&H Academic, 2006); Also see Kostenberger and O'Brien, *Salvation to the Ends of the Earth,* 32, 252; David Baker, *Two Testaments, One Bible* (Downers Grove, IL: IVP Academic, 2010), 242.

[69] The command, "Be fruitful" has turned into a promise: "I will make your fruitful." N.T. Wright, *The New Testament and the People of God* (Minneapolis: Fortress, 1992), 263. The word for "nation" is *goy* which is usually reserved for the world community excluding Israel, when used of Israel – it is often used in a pejorative manner (cf. Jud 2:20). The normal way of referring to Israel is *am*. This usage is probably to point to the later emergence of Israel as a geopolitical entity. See W. J. Dumbrell, "The Covenant With Abraham," *The Reformed Theological Review* 41.2 (May-August 1982), 43; Paul Williamson, *Sealed With an Oath* (Downers Grove, IL: InterVarsity Press, 2007), 82-83; T.D. Alexander, *From Paradise to the Promised Land,* 144.

[70] Our English translations often translate this phrase as "and you will be a blessing." This is a fine translation but the fact that it is an imperative is often missed. I prefer, "and you, be a blessing." See Christopher Wright, *The Mission of God,* 200-01.

C. All peoples will be blessed through you[71]

Here we have two goals:

1) To form Abraham into a great nation with land, offspring, and blessing

2) To bless all nations through Abraham's one great nation[72]

The mission of God catapults from here. Abraham and his family are blessed *in order* to be a blessing. As Christopher Wright observes, "We cannot speak biblically of the doctrine of election without insisting that it was never an end in itself but a means to the greater end of the ingathering of the nations. Election must be seen as missiological, not merely soteriological."[73] Abraham and his family are blessed *in order* to be mediators of blessing. Michael Goheen agrees, "Abraham's particular election is the instrument for the universal purpose of God with the whole world. Thus in the biblical story, privilege and responsibility, salvation and service, receiving, and mediating blessing, belong together in election. God's people are a "so that people": they are chosen *so that* they might know God's salvation and then invite all nations into it."[74]

---

[71] Wright, *Mission of God,* 200-01; see also Gentry and Wellum, *Kingdom Through Covenant,* 234.

[72] Paul R. Williamson, *Sealed With An Oath* (Downers Grove, IL: IVP, 2007), 79, 82.

[73] Wright, *The Mission of God,* 369. This is not meant to advocate a Barthian view of election where it is *merely* election unto service. It is both! To the pit with such false dichotomies that cause our theology to be reductionistic.

[74] Goheen, *A Light to the Nations,* 31.

The Abrahamic covenant has been called the original Great Commission.[75] The Great Commission can be seen as a Christological mutation of the original Abrahamic commission: "Go … and be a blessing … and all nations on earth will be blessed through you."[76] "That the nations of the world will find blessing through the descendants of Abraham is the central missionary motif of the Bible."[77]

Old Covenant

Before receiving the Law, Israel is given a programmatic statement for her vocation: "'You have seen what I did to the Egyptians and how I carried you on eagles' wings and brought you to Me. Now if you will listen to Me and carefully keep My covenant, you will be My own possession out of all the peoples, although all the earth is Mine, and you will be My kingdom of priests and My holy nation.' These are the words that you are to say to the Israelites" (Exod 19:4-6). In many ways, these verses are a restatement of Genesis 12:1-3.[78] As Abraham's offspring, Israel is blessed to be a

---

[75] Wilbert R. Shenk, "New Wineskins for New Wine: Toward a Post-Christendom Ecclesiology," *International Bulletin of Missionary Research* 29, no. 2 (April 2005): 73.

[76] Wright, *The Mission of God,* 213.

[77] Graeme Goldsworthy, "Biblical Theology and the Shape of Paul's Mission," in *The Gospel to the Nations: Perspectives on Paul's Mission*, eds. Peter Bolt and Mark Thompson (Downers Grove, IL: InterVarsity Press, 2000), 7-18.

[78] W.J. Dumbrell, *Covenant and Creation* (Carlisle: Paternoster, 1984), 89; Wright, *The Mission of God,* 225.

blessing.[79] They are to be a servant nation. God is totally committed to his mission of blessing the nations through the agency of Abraham's offspring,[80] or as N.T. Wright frequently puts it, God's "single-plan-through-Israel-for-the-world."[81]

Israel was called to be a display people, "embodying in its communal life God's original creational intention and eschatological goal for humanity ... an attractive sign before all nations of what God had intended in the beginning, and of the goal toward which he was moving: the restoration of all creation and human life from the corruption of sin."[82]

Israel was called to be a priestly kingdom, serving the world by being separate from it.[83] Her calling was funda-

---

[79] Wright writes, "The particularity of Israel here is intended to serve the universality of God's interest in the world. Israel's election serves God's mission." *The Mission of God,* 257.

[80] Wright, *The Mission of God,* 63.

[81] N.T. Wright, *Justification: God's Plan & Paul's Vision* (Downers Grove, IL: IVP Academic, 2009), 216.

[82] Goheen, *A Light to the Nations,* 25. Wright similarly notes, "The life of God's people is always turned outward to the watching nations, as priests are always turned toward their people as well as toward God." Wright, *The Mission of God,* 371.

[83] Andreas J. Kostenberger and Peter T. O'Brien, *Salvation to the Ends of the Earth: A Biblical Theology of Mission* (Downers Grove, IL: InterVarsity Press, 2001), 34; William J. Dumbrell, *Search for Order* (Eugene, OR: Wipf and Stock, 1994), 45; David Peterson, *Engaging with God: A Biblical Theology of Worship* (Downers Grove, IL: InterVarsity Press, 1992), 28.

mentally missiological![84]As a priesthood, the nation had the task of bringing the knowledge of God to the nations and bringing to the nations the means of atonement.[85] They were to represent what it looked like to live under the rule of God and fulfill Adam's mandate to expand his presence as his king-priests.[86] Of course, that is not to say that Israel was to

---

[84] Dempster, *Dominions and Dynasty,* 76, 149; Paul R. Williamson says, "The whole nation has thus inherited the responsibility formerly conferred on Abraham – that of mediating God's blessing to the nations of the earth ... Israel's election as Yahweh's 'special treasure' was not an end in itself, but a means to a much greater end. Thus understood, the goal of the Sinaitic covenant was the establishment of a special nation through which Yahweh could make himself known to all the families of the earth." *Sealed With an Oath: Covenant in God's Unfolding Purpose* (Downers Grove, IL: InterVarsity Press, 2007), 97; also see 114.

[85] Wright, *The Mission of God,* 331.

[86] Beale, *The Temple and the Church's Mission,* 118-21. Beale writes, "In this new creation Israel was to function as a kind of corporate Adam in their renewed Garden of Eden and spread out from there, reflecting God's glory in obedience to the commission of Genesis 1:28. History was starting over again, and Israel was the crown even of the human creation," 149-50. Later he summarizes: "Adam's purpose in that first garden-temple was to expand its boundaries until it circumscribed the earth, so that the earth would be completely filled with God's glorious presence. Adam's failure led, in time, to the re-establishment of the tabernacle and temple in Israel. Both were patterned after the model of Eden and were constructed to symbolize the entire cosmos in order to signify that Israel's purpose as a corporate Adam was to extend its borders by faithfully obeying God and spreading his glorious presence throughout the earth," 369; Also cf. Dumbrell, *Search for Order,* 45.

be involved in cross-cultural evangelism.[87] To say that Israel was to be a nation of evangelists and missionaries in a centrifugal manner goes beyond the biblical text. Israel was to be a light to the nations (Isa 49:6), witnessing "to the saving purposes of God by experiencing them and living according to them" in a centripetal manner.[88] As Beale notes, "They were to be mediators in spreading the light of God's tabernacling presence to the rest of the dark world."[89] As the story-line continues, Israel fails time and again in her vocational calling. Eventually, God raises up King David and promises him a son who will have an eternal kingdom. This is in fulfillment of the promise made to Abraham (Gen 12, 17:6), so that now the blessing for the many is mediated by the kingship of the one (Ps 72:17).[90] Israel, however, doesn't have the heart to obey (Deut 30:6; Ezek 36:26), and soon after the installment of the monarchy, she is in exile. Israel is eventually freed from exile, but things aren't the same as they were under Solomon's reign (Ezra 3:12). The Old Tes-

---

[87] Contra Walter C. Kaiser Jr., *Mission in the Old Testament* (Grand Rapids: Baker Books, 2000), 9-10, 22-24. Cf. Kostenberger, *Salvation to the Ends of the Earth*, 34-36, showing that Israel's role was to be centripetal, not centrifugal. See also Wright, *The Mission of God*, 331, 502ff, 523.

[88] Graeme L. Goldsworthy, "The Great Indicative: An Aspect of a Biblical Theology of Mission," *The Reformed Theological Review* 55, no. 1 (Jan-Apr 1996): 7.

[89] Beale, *The Temple and the Church's Mission*, 117. In Wright's words, "For Israel, it meant being different by reflecting the very different God that YHWH revealed himself to be, compared with other gods. Israel was to be as different from other nations as YHWH was different from other gods." Wright, *The Mission of God*, 363.

[90] Blaising and Bock, *Progressive Dispensationalism*, 166.

tament narrative ends with promises unfulfilled (Hag 2:9; Isa 65:17). A new covenant is needed (Jer 31:31-34; Ezek 36-37). The Old Testament ends with a whimper, not with a bang.[91] It ends with a question mark rather than an exclamation point.

New Covenant

Enter: King Jesus. The last Adam, the seed of the woman who crushes the serpent's head, the singular seed of Abraham, the Davidic King, the ascended Son of Man, the suffering servant who embodies Israel and through his death/resurrection/ascension, he brings blessing to the nations. Acts 3:25-26 combines the covenant with Abraham, David, and the Suffering Servant: "You are the sons of the prophets and of the covenant that God made with your ancestors, saying to Abraham, 'And all the families of the earth will be blessed through your offspring. God raised up His Servant and sent Him first to you to bless you by turning each of you from your evil ways'."

As prophesied, the Lord poured out his Spirit at Pentecost and formed his new covenant community. They are fully forgiven and indwelt by the empowering presence of God. They are "called out ones," commissioned to demonstrate in their living what it means to live under the rule of King Jesus.[92] We represent the reign of God[93] and are therefore a

---

[91] Dr. Bruce Ware is fond of pointing this out.

[92] Tim Chester and Steve Timmis, *Total Church: A Radical Reshaping around Gospel and Community* (Wheaton, IL: Crossway Books, 2008), 101.

[93] Hunsberger, "The Newbigin Gauntlet: Developing a Domestic Missiology for North America," 15.

contrast society,[94] an alternate community, resident aliens (1 Pet 2:11), which is simultaneously to be at home and a foreigner.[95] The new covenant community is called to be a peculiar people. With the onset of Christendom, the church lost its identity as being distinct from the world. They no longer embodied an alternative story and an alternative worldview, but imbibed idolatrous and imperial values. Would that this were only a 4th century issue! Today we must teach our people out of common cultural idols as well. The church is called to embody the gospel, but we will spend the rest of this book fleshing out seven different images of the church in the New Testament with an emphasis on the church's call to proclaim the gospel. What follows could also be described as "a biblical theology of the missional church."

---

[94] Keller, *Center Church*, 260.

[95] Goheen, *A Light to the Nations*, 7.

PART III –
IMAGES OF THE
MISSIONAL CHURCH

Great Commission People

The new covenant church is called to be a "Great Commission People." The famous text is Matthew 28:18-20. I will include the transliteration of a few important Greek words in order to show allusions to Old Testament passages: "Then Jesus came near and said to them, "All authority (*exousia*) has been given (*edōthē*) to Me in heaven and on earth. Go, therefore, and make disciples of all nations (*panta ta ethnē*), baptizing them in the name of the Father and of the Son and of the Holy Spirit, teaching them to observe everything I have commanded you. And remember, I am with you always, to the end of the age." Jesus has been given all authority. Here Jesus is echoing the all-important verses in Daniel 7. Notice the similar language used in the two passages: "I continued watching in the night visions, and I saw One like a son of man coming with the clouds of heaven. He approached the Ancient of Days and was escorted before Him. He was given authority (*edōthē autō exousia*) to rule, and glory, and a kingdom; so that those of every people, nation (*panta ta ethnē*), and language should serve Him. His dominion is an everlasting dominion (*exousia*) that will not pass away, and His kingdom is one that will not be destroyed."

In the Great Commission, we also see an allusion to Psalm 2, where we read of the enthronement of the Davidic King, the Christ: "I will declare the LORD's decree: He said to Me, 'You are My Son; today I have become Your Father. Ask of Me, and I will make the nations Your inheritance and the ends of the earth Your possession'." Jesus is the Danielic Son of Man who has been given all authority. He is the King. He is the Son of God. It is from this basis – the all inclusive authority of the ascended Son of Man – that the church is commissioned to make disciples, baptize, and teach.[96] Picking up on Christ's authority as the basis for the Great Commission, John Dickson coined what he calls the "mission equation:" If there is one Lord to whom all people belong and owe their allegiance, the people of that Lord must promote this reality everywhere."[97] Mission is the summons of the lordship of Christ.[98]

There is yet another allusion here to the Abraham narrative. Genesis 18:18 says, "Abraham is to become a great and powerful nation, and all the nations (_panta ta ethnē_) of the earth will be blessed through him." Christopher Wright says, "The words of Jesus to his disciples in Matthew 28:18-20, the so-called Great Commission, could be seen as a Christological mutation of the original Abrahamic commis-

---

[96] Though it is a conversation for another time, I must point out that in Daniel's programmatic vision, the Son of Man coming with the clouds is an ascension from earth to heaven, not the other way around. Allusion is also made to Isaiah 2:2-3: all nations (_panta ta ethnē_) will stream to the mountain of the Lord's house in the last days.

[97] John Dickson, _The Best Kept Secret of Christian Mission_ (Grand Rapids: Zondervan, 2010), 31, 35, 115.

[98] Johannes Blauw, _Missionary Nature of the Church_ (Cambridge: Lutterworth Press, 2003), 89.

sion – 'Go ... and be a blessing ... and all nations on earth will be blessed through you'."[99]

This commission does not end with the disciples, but rather, the church as a whole inherits this missionary commission.[100] In many ways, the "Great Commission is the command of the new covenant."[101] John Frame writes, "The Great Commission must be the focus of everything the church does. Indeed, it must be the focus of the life of every believer."[102] Frame goes on to say, "All the New Testament statements of the goal of the Christian life focus on redemption, on bringing unbelievers into the kingdom. So, all the work of the church is missional."[103]

As noted above, God is a missionary God. He sends the Son and through the Son sends the Spirit and the Son sends his body in the power of the Spirit. In John 20:21, we read: "Jesus said to them again, 'Peace to you! As the Father has sent Me, I also send you'."[104] Johannine scholar, Andreas Köstenberger writes, "A proper understanding of John's

---

[99] Wright, *The Mission of God,* 213.

[100] See Robert L. Plummer, "The Great Commission in the New Testament," *The Southern Baptist Journal of Theology* 9, no. 4 (Winter 2005): 5, 9.

[101] Wright, *The Mission of God,* 354.

[102] Frame, *Salvation Belongs to the Lord,* 251.

[103] Ibid., 256.

[104] Regarding the so-called Johannine Pentecost following this verse (John 20:22), it should be seen as a prolepsis of Pentecost. It is an enacted parable pointing forward to the full endowment to come. See Allison, *Sojourners and Strangers,* 142; Carson, *John,* 655; Hastings, *Missional God, Missional Church,* 28.

Trinitarian mission theology ought to lead the church to *understand its mission in Trinitarian terms*, that is, as originating in and initiated by the Father (the 'one who sent' Jesus), as redemptively grounded and divinely mediated by Jesus the Son (the 'Sent One' turned sender, John 20:21), and as continued and empowered by the Spirit, the 'other helping presence,' the Spirit of truth."[105]

Jesus' mission is continued and is effective through the disciples,[106] who are drawn into the mission of the Father and Son.[107] Christ has sent us. We are *sent* people. Again, Köstenberger poignantly writes, "For John there is no separate class of 'missionaries': *all* believers are sent."[108]

The Inter-Advental People

Have you ever thought about why there are two comings of the Messiah? Why did God not simply wrap it all up in the first coming? I think *part* of the answer is that God wanted to form a faithful end-time community and use it as his instrument for the completion of his mission – just like from the beginning and throughout redemptive history. The church is the eschatological community, the people of the

---

[105] Andreas J. Köstenberger, "John's Trinitarian Mission Theology," *The Southern Baptist Journal of Theology* 9, no. 4 (Winter 2005): 27. In this same journal issue, see Robert L. Plummer, "The Great Commission in the New Testament," 7.

[106] D.A. Carson, "The Gospel According to John", *The Pillar New Testament Commentary* (Grand Rapids: Eerdmans, 1991), 649.

[107] Andreas J. Köstenberger, "John", *Baker Exegetical Commentary on the New Testament* (Grand Rapids: Baker Academic, 2004), 573.

[108] Andreas Köstenberger, *The Missions of Jesus and the Disciples According to the Fourth Gospel* (Grand Rapids: Eerdmans, 1998), 198.

future, "the preview of a new day, a new world."[109] The blood-bought new covenant community is the sign, fore-taste, and instrument of the kingdom of God.[110] The church is both the result of mission and the instrument of mission;[111] she is formed *by* mission and *for* mission.[112]

We live in the overlap of the ages as the community upon whom the end of the ages has come (1 Cor 10:11). This aspect of our identity must be recovered. Gordon Fee writes, "At a recent coffee hour with students in the Regent College atrium, one student asked, 'If you were to return to the pastoral ministry, what would you do [meaning, How would you go about it? What would you emphasize]?' My answer was immediate: 'No matter how long it might take, I would set about with a single passion to help a local body of believers recapture the New Testament church's understanding of itself as an eschatological community'."[113] Amen. Let's follow this example.

This time between the times is *for mission*. The last days began with the resurrection of Christ and the last days are missionary days (Acts 2:17; Heb 1:1). The present era is defined by witness.[114] The inter-advental period is the period

---

[109] Goheen, *A Light to the Nations*, 3.

[110] Van Gelder, *The Essence of the Church*, 99.

[111] Goheen, *A Light to the Nations*, 174.

[112] Chester and Timmis, *Total Church*, 103.

[113] Gordon D. Fee, *Paul, the Spirit, and the People of God* (Peabody, MA: Hendrickson, 1996), 49; cf. 190.

[114] Goheen, *A Light to the Nations*, 126; Köstenberger and O'Brien, *Salvation to the Ends of the Earth*, 269; Craig G. Bartholomew and Michael

of mission and eschatological gathering.[115] It is for the gathering of Jews and Gentiles into the Kingdom. Christ has commissioned his followers to be fishers of men, calling in the exiles (Jer 16:14-18 in Matt 4:18-19).[116] Newbigin says that to miss missionary obedience as the main point of the time between the times is to have a false eschatology.[117] O'Brien and Köstenberger are right to say that "Mission is the church's primary task between Christ's first coming and his return."[118]

W. Goheen, *The Drama of Scripture: Finding Our Place in the Biblical Story* (Grand Rapids: Baker Academic, 2004), 13.

[115] Yves Congar says "The time of the Church is essentially a time of mission," *I Believe in the Holy Spirit*, (New York: The Crossroad Publishing Company, 1983), 58. Alan J. Thompson writes, "The spread of the Word through proclamation, planting and strengthening local churches, in the midst of suffering, therefore, dominates Luke's instruction for Christian readers like Theophilus about what is to characterize the people of God in this new stage in salvation history." *The Acts of the Risen Lord* (Downers Grove, IL: InterVarsity Press, 2011), 88.

[116] Peter J. Gentry and Stephen J. Wellum, *Kingdom Through Covenant* (Wheaton, IL: Crossway, 2012), 489-90.

[117] Newbigin, *The Household of God* (New York: Friendship Press, 1953), 153.

[118] Köstenberger and O'Brien, *Salvation to the Ends of the Earth: A Biblical Theology of Mission*, 108. Millard Erickson writes, "The one topic emphasized in both accounts of Jesus' last words to his disciples is evangelism. In Matthew 28:19 he instructs them, 'Go therefore and make disciples of all nations.' In Acts 1:8 he says, 'But you will receive power when the Holy Spirit has come upon you; and you shall be my witnesses in Jerusalem and in all Judea and Samaria and to the end of the earth.' This was the final point Jesus made to his disciples. It appears that he regarded evangelism as the very reason for their

Body of Christ

Another image of the church with missional implications is the church as the body of Christ (1 Cor 12:27; Eph 4:12). We are the manifestation of the risen Christ on earth.[119] That obviously means that the body should not be dissimilar from the head. The church is a hermeneutic of the gospel, to use Newbigin's language. He writes,

> I have come to feel that the primary reality of which we have to take account in seeking for a Christian impact on public life is the Christian congregation. How is it possible that the gospel should be credible, that people should come to believe that the power which has the last word in human affairs is represented by a man hanging on a cross? I am suggesting that the only answer, the only hermeneutic of the gospel, is a congregation of men and women who believe it and live by it. I am, of course, not denying the importance of the many activities by which we seek to challenge public life with the gospel – evangelistic campaigns, distribution of Bibles and Christian literature, conferences, and even books such as this one. But I am saying that these are all secondary, and that they have power to accomplish their purpose only as they are rooted in and lead back to a believing community.[120]

If you want to know what Jesus looks like, look at his people.[121] The church is to imitate Christ by loving like he has loved us. Jesus said, "I give you a new command: Love

---

being." Millard J. Erickson, *Introducing Christian Doctrine* (Grand Rapids: Baker Academic, 2001), 347.

[119] Goheen, *A Light to the Nations,* 173.

[120] Lesslie Newbigin, *The Gospel in a Pluralist Society* (London: SPCK, 1989), 227.

[121] Ibid., 223-33.

one another. Just as I have loved you, you must also love one another. By this all people will know that you are My disciples, if you have love for one another" (John 13:34-35). The invisible God is made visible through the Christ-like love of the people of God (1 John 4:20-21).[122] Cruciform love is *the* fundamental virtue of the people of God.[123] Jesus forms a community around himself which functions as the continuation of his own presence on earth.[124] We are the body of Christ.

Priesthood of All Believers

The basic New Testament truth of the priesthood of every believer was rediscovered at the Reformation, but in too many churches it is still only an abstract truth and hasn't worked itself out in practical ways.[125] Too many Christians still think of ministry in terms of the pastor/priest. I am very thankful for the recent literature, much of it missionally-focused that teaches otherwise. As Tim Chester and Steve Timmis write in their superb book, *Total Church*, "Most gospel ministry involves *ordinary people doing ordinary things with gospel intentionality.*"[126] I think many churches aren't

---

[122] Chester and Timmis, *Total Church*, 10, 59.

[123] For more on cruciform love, see part two of my *Theological Foundations for New Covenant Ethics* (Frederick, MD: New Covenant Media, 2013).

[124] J.R. Daniel Kirk, *Jesus Have I Loved, but Paul?* (Grand Rapids: Baker Academic, 2011), 60.

[125] Surprisingly, one of the best treatments of this topic is found in Hans Kung, *The Church* (New York: Burns and Oates, 1968), 363-87.

[126] Chester and Timmis, *Total Church,* 63. Chester and Timmis' book is fantastic, as well as Colin Marshall and Tony Payne, *The Trellis and the*

thriving because they function as if there were the priesthood of one rather than of all. We need to take an axe to the clergy/laity distinction and activate our "ordinary" people in many "ordinary" ways, one of them being as informal missionaries with gospel intentionality in their own context.

Wilbert Shenk writes, "There is no biblical or theological basis for the territorial distinction between mission and evangelism. To accede to this dichotomy is to invite the church to 'settle in' and be at home."[127] This false distinction has been harmful to our doctrine of the church.[128] We must push all to recognize that all are missionaries to the context in which God has sovereignly placed us.[129] We have to help our people think as missionaries wherever they are. When you mention "mission" to most people, they think of people "over there" and merely feel guilty for not praying for them or sending checks frequently enough.[130]

Part of our task, then, is to broaden their understanding of ministry. Most of their ministry will involve ordinary things. Too often a person thinks because they can't preach a

---

Vine: The Ministry Mind-Shift that Changes Everything (Australia: Matthias Media, 2009). Also see Keller, *Center Church,* 279-81.

[127] Wilbert R. Shenk, "The Culture of Modernity as a Missionary Challenge," in *The Church Between Gospel & Culture: The Emerging Mission in North America,* eds. George R. Hunsberger and Craig Van Gelder (Grand Rapids: Eerdmans, 1996), 78.

[128] Stetzer, Planting New Churches, 28.

[129] Stetzer, Breaking the Missional Code, 3.

[130] George R. Hunsberger, "The Newbigin Gauntlet: Developing a Domestic Missiology for North America," in Hunsberger and Van Gelder, eds., *The Church Between Gospel and Culture,* 4.

sermon or sing a solo, or do something up "on stage," they aren't useful for God's kingdom. They need to grasp their calling as priests in God's world. What do priests do? They work in service to God in behalf of the people (Heb 5:1). Priests mediate the presence of God to the world.

First Peter 2:9 reads, "But you are a chosen race, a royal priesthood, a holy nation, a people for His possession, so that you may proclaim the praises of the One who called you out of darkness into His marvelous light." Here Peter applies Israel's titles to the church. It is not that the church is replacing Israel, but fulfilling her vocation via union with Christ. Israel is being purified and reconstituted. Holy priests represent God to the world.[131] Van Gelder notes, "The church stands at the crossroads between God and the world."[132]

Temple

The church as the temple of God has vast missional implications. As mentioned above, Adam and Eve were commissioned to subdue and rule over the earth, extending the boundaries of the garden-temple until the whole earth was Eden-like.[133] A full-orbed biblical theology of the temple must trace the theme from Eden to the Tabernacle, then Temple to Jesus,[134] then to his body – both individually and corporately, and finally the new earth.

---

[131] Hastings, *Missional God*, 13.

[132] Van Gelder, *The Essence of the Church*, 86.

[133] Beale, *The Temple and the Church's Mission*, 81-82, 85.

[134] As NT scholar David Peterson notes, "The glorified Lord Jesus is the new point of contact between heaven and earth for people of every

Pentecost (Acts 2) is the inauguration of the church as the Temple. The Spirit's descent is God's presence returning to the Temple, which is now defined around his people.[135] The people of God – the church – are the end time Temple. Further evidence for this comes from Peter's quotation of Isaiah 2 in his Pentecost sermon. He quotes Joel 2:28-32 in Acts 2:17-21, but adds the phrase "in the last days" (*en tais eschatais hēmerais*) that is not found in Joel. This exact phrase is only found in one other place in the Greek Old or New Testaments: Isaiah 2:2. This is significant. Isaiah 2:2-3 reads, "In the last days the mountain of the LORD's house will be established at the top of the mountains and will be raised above the hills. All nations will stream to it, and many peoples will come and say, 'Come, let us go up to the mountain of the LORD, to the house of the God of Jacob. He will teach us about His ways so that we may walk in His paths.' For instruction will go out of Zion and the word of the LORD from Jerusalem." The end-time temple that the nations are streaming to is the church on mission in the new covenant. The mountain of the Lord is being raised above the hills. As we witness and God adds to his people, the presence of God expands on earth – the temple grows. Therefore the church is the temple and is called to the task of "temple-building." As Christopher Wright notes, "Mission then may be com-

---

race without distinction." Peterson, *Engaging with God*, 143. Also cf. Beale, *The Temple and the Church's Mission*, 176-200.

[135] G.K. Beale, *A New Testament Biblical Theology* (Grand Rapids: Baker Academic, 2011), 593; idem, *The Temple and the Church's Mission*, 201.

pared to building the dwelling place of God and inviting the nations to come on home."[136]

Apostolic

The church is to be *doubly* apostolic. Yes, the church's new covenant constitution is the written Word of God, that is, founded on the Apostle's teaching, but the church is also apostolic in that it is *sent.*[137] Apostle means "sent one." As Craig Van Gelder writes, "The basic image of the church as apostolic conveys that the church is sent into the world authoritatively by God to participate fully in his redemptive work."[138]

Acts 29

The book of Acts seems to have an unfinished ending, which propels the post-Acts churches in their own mission.[139] There Paul is openly and actively preaching in Rome, indicating that the gospel of the kingdom is set to move

---

[136] Wright, *The Mission of God*, 340. On the concluding page of his superb study of the temple, G.K. Beale writes, "The main point of this book is that our task as the covenant community, the church is to be God's temple, so filled with his glorious presence that we expand and fill the earth with that presence until God finally accomplishes the goal completely at the end of time! This is our common mission." *The Temple and the Church's Mission*, 402.

[137] George R. Hunsberger, "Missional Vocation: Called and Sent to Represent the Reign of God," in *Missional Church: A Vision for the Sending of the Church in North America*, ed. Darrell Guder (Grand Rapids: Eerdmans, 1998), 83.

[138] Van Gelder, *The Essence of the Church*, 51; cf. 125.

[139] Allison, *Sojourners and Strangers,* 143-44. See the intriguing parallel with the end of 2 Kings argued by James A. Sanders, "Isaiah in Luke," *Interpretation* 36 (1982):147-48.

from the center of the Empire to all its parts. The mission has begun in Christ and his apostles. In his gospel, Luke told Theophilus "about all that Jesus began to do and teach" (Acts 1:1). Jesus began the mission and told the early church that they had been made "a light for the Gentiles to bring salvation to the ends of the earth" (Acts 13:47). Mission was still being accomplished. The story of Acts continues and will not come to an end until Christ returns and resurrects his saints and his cosmos.[140]

---

[140] Bartholomew and Goheen, *The Drama of Scripture*, 195-96.

CONCLUSION

So we have seen that God is the missional God who is working out his purposes from creation to new creation and he has formed his people to be the means he uses to accomplish his mission. Every Christian needs to view themselves as "sent" by the triune God to their particular context. I submit that this way of thinking is largely absent today and if recovered will do much to help people live more fulfilling lives, not focused on self but others, and will certainly aid in expanding the kingdom of God and bringing glory to our great God. I would like to conclude with six marks of a missional church from Tim Keller:

1. The church must confront society's idols.

2. The church must contextualize skillfully and communicate in the vernacular.

3. The church must equip people in mission in every area of their lives.

4. The church must be a counterculture for the common good.

5. The church must itself be contextualized and should expect nonbelievers, inquirers, and seekers to be involved in most aspects of the church's life and ministry.

6. The church must practice unity.[141]

---

[141] Keller, *Center Church*, 274. Lesslie Newbigin lists the following six ingredients for a missional church: "1.a new apologetic (that takes on the so-called neutrality of secular reason), 2. the teaching of the king-

---

dom of God (that God wants not only to save souls but heal the whole creation), 3. earning the right to be heard through willingness to serve others sacrificially, 4. equipping the laity to bring the implications of their faith into their public calling and so transform culture, 5. a countercultural church community, 6. a unified church that shows the world an overcoming of denominational divisions, 7. a global church in which the older Western churches listen to the non-Western churches, 8. courage." "Can the West Be Converted?," _International Bulletin of Missionary Research_ 11, no. 1 (January 1987): 2-7, quoted in Keller, _Center Church,_ 254.

soli deo gloria

BIBLIOGRAPHY

Alexander, T. Desmond. *From Eden to the New Jerusalem*. Downers Grove, IL: InterVarsity Press, 2008.

Allison, Gregg R. *Sojourners and Strangers: The Doctrine of the Church*. Wheaton, IL: Crossway, 2012.

Armstrong, John H. *Your Church is Too Small*. Grand Rapids: Zondervan, 2010.

Baker, David. *Two Testaments, One Bible*. Downers Grove, IL: IVP Academic, 2010.

Bartholomew, Craig G. and Michael W. Goheen. *The Drama of Scripture: Finding Our Place in the Biblical Story*. Grand Rapids: Baker Academic, 2004.

Beale, G.K. "Eden, the Temple, and the Church's Mission in the New Creation," *JETS 48.1* (March 2005).

_____. *A New Testament Biblical Theology*. Grand Rapids: Baker Academic, 2011.

_____. *The Temple and the Church's Mission.* Downers Grove, IL: InterVarsity Press, 2004.

Belcher, Jim. *Deep Church: A Third Way Beyond Emerging and Traditional*. Downers Grove, IL: IVP Books, 2009.

Blaising, Craig A. and Darrell Bock. *Progressive Dispensation-alsim.* Grand Rapids: Baker Books, 2000.

Blauw, Johannes. *The Missionary Nature of the Church.* Cambridge: Lutterworth Press, 2003.

Bosch, David J. *Believing in the Future: Toward a Missiology of Western Culture.* Valley Forge: Trinity Press International, 1995.

_____. *Transforming Mission: Paradigm Shifts in Theology of Mission.* Maryknoll, NY: Orbis Books, 1991.

Brunner, Emil. *The Word and the World.* London: Student Christian Movement Press, 1931.

Carson, D.A. *The Gospel According to John.* The Pillar New Testament Commentary. Grand Rapids: Eerdmans, 1991.

_____. *Becoming Conversant with the Emerging Church: Understanding a Movement and Its Implications.* Grand Rapids: Zondervan, 2005.

_____. *The Gagging of God: Christianity Confronts Pluralism.* Grand Rapids: Zondervan, 1996.

_____. ed. *Telling The Truth.* Grand Rapids: Zondervan, 2000.

Chester, Tim and Steve Timmis. *Total Church: A Radical Reshaping around Gospel and Community.* Wheaton, IL: Crossway Books, 2008.

Claiborne, Shane and Chris Haw. *Jesus For President*. Grand
   Rapids: Zondervan, 2008.

Congar, Yves. *I Believe in the Holy Spirit*. New York: The
   Crossroad Publishing Company, 1983.

Dempster, Stephen. *Dominion and Dynasty*. Downers Grove,
   IL: InterVarsity Press, 2003.

DeYoung, Kevin and Greg Gilbert. *What is the Mission of the
   Church?*. Wheaton, IL: Crossway, 2011.

DeYoung, Kevin and Ted Kluck. *Why We're Not Emergent*.
   Chicago: Moody, 2008.

Dickson, John. *The Best Kept Secret of Christian Mission*. Grand
   Rapids: Zondervan, 2010.

Driscoll, Mark. *The Radical Reformission: Reaching Out Without Selling Out*. Grand Rapids: Zondervan, 2004.

_____. *Confessions of a Reformission Rev*. Grand Rapids:
   Zondervan, 2006.

Dumbrell, William J. *The Search for Order*. Eugene, OR: Wiph
   and Stock, 1994.

_____. *Covenant and Creation*. Carlisle, PA: Paternoster,
   1984.

Erickson, Millard J. *Introducing Christian Doctrine*. Grand
   Rapids: Baker Academic, 2001.

Fee, Gordon D. *Paul, the Spirit, and the People of God*. Peabody, MA: Hendrickson, 1996.

Frame, John M. *Salvation Belongs to the Lord: An Introduction to Systematic Theology*. Phillipsburg, NJ: P & R Publishing, 2006.

Franke, John R. *The Character of Theology: An Introduction to Its Nature, Task, and Purpose*. Grand Rapids: Baker Academic, 2005.

Frost, Michael, and Alan Hirsch. *The Shaping of Things to Come: Innovation and Mission for the 21st-Century Church*. Peabody, MA: Hendrickson, 2003.

Gentry, Peter J. "Kingdom Through Covenant: Humanity as the Divine Image," *The Southern Baptist Journal of Theology* 12.1 (Spring 2008).

_____. and Stephen J. Wellum. *Kingdom Through Covenant*. Wheaton, IL: Crossway, 2012.

Gibbs, Eddie. *ChurchNext: Quantum Changes in How We Do Ministry*. Downers Grove, IL: InterVarsity Press, 2000.

Goheen, Michael W. *A Light to the Nations: The Missional Church and the Biblical Story*. Grand Rapids: Baker Academic, 2011.

Goldsworthy, Graeme. "Biblical Theology and the Shape of Paul's Mission." In *The Gospel to the Nations: Perspectives on Paul's Mission*. Edited by Peter Bolt and Mark

Thompson. Downers Grove, IL: InterVarsity Press, 2000.

_____. "The Great Indicative: An Aspect of a Biblical Theology of Mission. *The Reformed Theological Review* 55, no. 1 (Jan-April 1996).

Gonzàles, Justo L. *The Story of Christianity.* Vol. 1. Peabody, MA: Prince Press, 2005.

Guder, Darrell L., "Missional Church: From Sending to Being Sent." In *Missional Church: A Vision for the Sending of the Church in North America*, ed. Darrell L. Guder, 1-17. Grand Rapids: Eerdmans, 1998.

_____., ed. *Missional Church: A Vision for the Sending of the Church in North America.* Grand Rapids: Eerdmans, 1998.

_____. "Missional Theology for a Missionary Church." *Journal for Preachers* 22, no. 1 (Advent 1998): 3-11.

Hastings, Ross. *Missional God, Missional Church.* Downers Grove: IVP Academic, 2012.

Horton, Michael. *The Gospel Commission.* Grand Rapids: Baker Books, 2011.

Hunsberger, George R. "The Newbigin Gauntlet." In *The Church Between Gospel & Culture: The Emerging Mission in North America*, eds. George R. Hunsberger and Craig Van Gelder, 3-25. Grand Rapids: Eerdmans, 1996.

_____. "Missional Vocation: Called and Sent to Represent the Reign of God." In *Missional Church: A Vision for the Sending of the Church in North America*, ed. Darrell L. Guder, 77-109. Grand Rapids: Eerdmans, 1998.

_____. "Sizing Up the Shape of the Church." In *The Church Between Gospel & Culture: The Emerging Mission in North America*, eds. George R. Hunsberger and Craig Van Gelder, 333-46. Grand Rapids: Eerdmans, 1996.

Hunsberger, George R. and Craig Van Gelder, eds. *The Church Between Gospel and Culture*. Grand Rapids: Eerdmans, 1996.

Keller, Timothy. *Center Church*. Grand Rapids: Zondervan, 2012.

Kimball, Dan. *The Emerging Church*. Grand Rapids: Zondervan, 2003.

Kirk, J. Andrew. "Mission in the West," In *A Scandalous Prophet: The Way of Mission after Newbigin*, eds. Thomas F. Foust, George R. Hunsberger, J. Andrew Kirk, and Werner Ustorf, 115-27. Grand Rapids: Eerdmans, 2002.

Kirk, J.R. Daniel. *Jesus Have I Loved, but Paul?* Grand Rapids: Baker Academic, 2011.

Kostenberger, Andreas J and Peter T. O'Brien. *Salvation to the Ends of the Earth: A Biblical Theology of Mission*. Downers Grove, IL: InterVarsity Press, 2001.

Kostenberger, Andreas J. *The Missions of Jesus & the Disciples According to the Fourth Gospel*. Grand Rapids: Eerdmans, 1998.

_____. *John*. Baker Exegetical Commentary on the New Testament. Grand Rapids: Baker Academic, 2004.

_____. "John's Trinitarian Mission Theology." *The Southern Baptist Journal of Theology* 9, no. 4 (Winter 2005): 14-33.

Kreider, Alan and Eleanor Kreider. *Worship & Mission After Christendom*. Scottdale, PA: Herald Press, 2011.

Kung, Hans. *The Church*. New York: Burns and Oates, 1968.

Litfin, Bryan M. "Eusebius on Constantine: Truth and Hagiography at the Milvian Bridge." *JETS* 55, no. 4 (December 2012): 773-92.

Littell, Franklin H. *The Anabaptist View of the Church*. Paris, AK: The Baptist Standard Bearer, 1958.

Marshall, Colin and Tony Payne. *The Trellis and the Vine*. Australia: Matthias Media, 2009.

McGrath, Alister E. *Historical Theology*. Malden, MA: Black-well, 1998.

McLaren, Brian D. *A Generous Orthodoxy*. Grand Rapids: Zondervan, 2004.

Mouw, Richard J. "The Missionary Location of the North American Churches." In *Confident Witness--Changing World: Rediscovering the Gospel in North America*, ed. Craig Van Gelder, 3-15. Grand Rapids: Eerdmans, 1999.

Murray, Stuart. *The Naked Anabaptist: The Bare Essentials of a Radical Faith*. Scottdale, PA: Herald Press, 2010.

Newbigin, Lesslie. "Can the West Be Converted?." *International Bulletin of Missionary Research* 11, no. 1 (January 1987).

_____. *Foolishness to the Greeks: The Gospel and Western Culture*. Grand Rapids: Eerdmans, 1986.

_____. *Household of God*. New York: Friendship Press, 1954.

_____. *One Body, One Gospel, One World: The Christian Mission Today*. New York: International Missionary Council, 1960.

_____. *The Gospel in a Pluralist Society*. London: SPCK, 1989.

_____. *The Other Side of 1984*. Geneva: World Council of Churches, 1983.

_____. *Trinitarian Faith and Today's Mission*. Richmond, VA: John Knox Press, 1964.

Peterson, David. *Engaging with God*. Downers Grove, IL: InterVarsity Press, 1992.

Piper, John. *Let the Nations Be Glad!: The Supremacy of God in Missions*. Grand Rapids: Baker Books, 1993.

Plummer, Robert L. "Imitation of Paul and the Church's Missionary Role in 1 Corinthians." *Journal of the Evangelical Theological Society* 44, no. 2 (June 2001): 219-35.

_____. *Paul's Understanding of the Church's Mission*. Waynesboro, GA: Paternoster, 2006.

_____. "The Great Commission in the New Testament." *The Southern Baptist Journal of Theology* 9, no. 4 (Winter 2005): 4-11.

Richter, Sandra L. *The Epic of Eden: A Christian Entry into the Old Testament*. Downers Grove, IL: IVP Academic, 2008.

Shenk, Wibert R. "The Culture of Modernity as a Missionary Challenge." In *The Church Between Gospel & Culture: The Emerging Mission in North America*, eds. George R. Hunsberger and Craig Van Gelder, 69-78. Grand Rapids: Eerdmans, 1996.

_____. "Missionary Encounter with Culture." *International Bulletin of Missionary Research* 15 (July 1991): 104-09.

_____."New Wineskins for New Wine: Toward a Post-Christendom Ecclesiology." *International Bulletin of Missionary Research* 29, no. 2 (April 2005): 73-79.

Stephen J. Wellum, "Baptism and the Relationship between the Covenants." In *Believer's Baptism,* eds. Thomas R. Schreiner and Shawn D. Wright. Nashville: B&H Academic, 2006.

Stetzer, Ed and David Putman. *Breaking the Missional Code: Your Church Can Become a Missionary in Your Community*. Nashville: Broadman & Holman, 2006.

_____.*Planting New Churches in a Postmodern Age*. Nashville: Broadman & Holman, 2003.

Stott, John. *Motives and Methods in Evangelism*. Leicester, UK: Inter-Varsity, 1962.

Sweeney, Douglas A. *The American Evangelical Story*. Grand Rapids: Baker, 2005.

Thompson, Alan J. *The Acts of the Risen Lord.* Downers Grove, IL: InterVarsity Press, 2011.

Van Engen, Charles. *God's Missionary People: Rethinking the Purpose of the Local Church*. Grand Rapids: Baker Book House, 1991.

Van Gelder, Craig. "Defining the Center—Finding the Boundaries." In *The Church Between Gospel & Culture: The Emerging Mission in North America,* eds. George R.

Hunsberger and Craig Van Gelder, 26-51. Grand Rapids: Eerdmans, 1996.

_____. *The Essence of the Church: A Community Created by the Spirit*. Grand Rapids: Baker, 2000.

Veith, Jr., Gene Edward. *Postmodern Times: A Christian Guide to Contemporary Thought and Culture*. Wheaton: Crossway Books, 1994.

Wells, David. *Above All Earthly Pow'rs: Christ in a Postmodern World*. Grand Rapids: Eerdmans, 2005.

Williamson, Paul R. *Sealed With an Oath: Covenant in God's Unfolding Purpose*. Downers Grove, IL: InterVarsity Press, 2007.

Wright, Christopher J.H. *The Mission of God*. Downers Grove, IL: IVP Academic, 2006.

Wright, N.T. *The New Testament and the People of God*. Minneapolis: Fortress Press, 1992.

_____. *Justification: God's Plan & Paul's Vision*. Downers Grove, IL: IVP Academic, 2009.

Made in the USA
Charleston, SC
02 June 2015